CW00556147

THINGS MY CHILDREN THINK I'M WRONG ABOUT

NIC AUBURY

Bedford Square
Publishers

Also by Nic Aubury

Ignore It All and Hope It Goes Away:
Poems for Modern Life

for my sons and my parents

First published in the UK in 2024 by
Bedford Square Publishers Ltd, London, UK

bedfordsquarepublishers.co.uk
@bedsqpublishers

A CIP catalogue record for this book
is available from the British Library.

ISBN
978-1-83501-121-8 (Hardback)
978-1-83501-122-5 (eBook)

2 4 6 8 10 9 7 5 3 1

Typeset in Celeste by
Palimpsest Book Production Ltd, Falkirk, Stirlingshire

Printed in Great Britain by CPI Group (UK) Ltd, Croydon CR0 4YY

Contents

Family

Matters

———

Same Difference

Determined to avoid the fate of waking up one day
to find that we've become our dad or mum,
we make ourselves the people who our kids will be afraid
of waking up to find that they've become.

Three Wishes

'What, anything at all?' the parent said.
'Your wish is my command', the genie bowed.
'Well, really, I'd just like to go to bed
and sleep right through', the parent mused aloud.
The next thing that the parent could recall
was waking after eight unbroken hours,
while feeling that no time had passed at all,
and, understanding now the genie's powers,
the parent's rested mind began to spin
with giddy thoughts of wishes two and three.
So, rubbing at the dull and dented tin,
the parent set the grateful genie free
and said, before he'd risen from his bow:
'Another two of those. I'll take both now.'

Hot or Not

When choosing an outfit, our offspring pay heed
to the stuff that they've seen on their Instagram feed,
to advice from their friends, to their own inhibitions,
but not to observable weather conditions.

Two-Part Harmony

My parents in their daily speech
avoided altercations
by simply having one half each
of separate conversations.

The Bad Parent's Haiku

There are lots of ways
to deal with a teenager.
All of them are wrong.

Depending

The seventeen-to-twenty-fives
are grown-ups 'til the bill arrives.

What?

A dozen lorries, maybe more, a cargo ship or plane
and several hundred postal sacks would easily be fillable
by possibly a quarter or a fifth of the disdain
my children can deliver in a single monosyllable.

What Goes Around

I'm sure they would be gratified
to know, now I'm a dad,
I'm fully on my parents' side
in all the rows we had.

The Father of Philosophy

To learn that there was nothing that he knew
took Socrates – the wisest of his peers –
a lifetime's work, when all I had to do
was have some kids and wait for thirteen years.

The Second-Favourite Parents' Club

As I and every member of our club have always known,
whose other halves are fêted *in excelsis*,
we'd rather be the second-favourite parent to our own
than number one to anybody else's.

Man's Stupidest Friend

He skitters and skids to a halt, and I know
that the wagging and whining won't stop
and will grow more insistent, in fact, 'til I throw
the ball he refuses to drop.

World's Median Dad

for Brian

Of all the dads, I know I'm not the best,
in spite of what the mug you bought might say.
I'm somewhere in the middle, I'd suggest –

not terrible, but sometimes slightly stressed
with work and too preoccupied to play.
Of all the dads I know, I'm not the best

at football, as I'm sure you would attest,
but if I go in goal, then that's okay.
I'm somewhere in the middle, I'd suggest,

at building dens – although you were impressed
that time I made a swing on holiday.
Of all the dads – I know – I'm not the best

at cooking, and I'm pretty badly dressed,
but sometimes not unfunny, in my way.
I'm somewhere in the middle, I'd suggest,

at most things, but compared to all the rest
I always feel I've won on Father's Day.
Of all the dads, I know I'm not the best;
I'm somewhere in the middle, I'd suggest.

One Less Thing

For dads, self-deprecation, I assure you,
is redundant:
the deprecation's taken care of for you,
and abundant.

The Parent Small Print

It's apparent that my kids have not appreciated quite
that it doesn't really count as interfering if I'm right.

Polonian

If I were more convincing and
my children more convincible
then this would be the wisdom I'd impart:
be ready to abandon an
opinion, not a principle,
and learn to tell those different things apart.

Warp and Weft

The past has got a funny way,
the more your children grow,
of feeling both like yesterday
and several lives ago.

Universal

If all the stars and planets that exist
had names, and all those names were written out,
it wouldn't be as long as half the list
of things my children think I'm wrong about.

Empty Nest Paradox

With parenting (the most arcane
of any grown-up art)
it's only once you've finished that
you know enough to start.

Affairs

of the

Heart

———

True Romance

You're not convinced the stars align to set two hearts aflame.
You don't believe that destiny ensures we always meet
our perfect other half. You think it's like that party game,
where, once the music's stopped, you take the nearest empty seat,

though any of the other chairs would equally have done,
and might have been more comfortable. But, even if that's true,
and people are deluded if they think they've found the one,
I'm happy that the nearest bum without a seat was you.

Wastepaper Augury

He whispers to himself: 'If this goes in,
she'll leave that stupid oaf and marry me.'
He watches as it arcs beyond the bin,
then, fetching it, he mutters: 'Best of three.'

Cold War

I only need to sniff a bit or cough
from somewhere in your earshot, and I'm told
in no uncertain terms just how pissed off
you'll be if I should dare give you my cold.
I'm tempted to explain that this is not
my cold, which you assume I want to spread
as part of some great spouse-infecting plot;
that I am not some viral fountainhead;
that this is someone else's cold, not mine,
which they were kind enough to pass my way;
that, given that I'm manifestly fine,
in any case you might just be okay.
I don't, of course, but note with private glee
you're accidentally drinking from my tea.

Fact and Friction

'I guess it's subjective', you say in the end
when you think that we've argued too long,
which means, more or less, I'm obliged to pretend
that it's fine that you're utterly wrong.

Cheshire Limerick

There was an old fellow from Cholmondeley
whose wife was exceedingly colmondeley.
'The problem I find
is that when I'm inclined
she is anything but', he said glolmondeley.

Conditionally Yours

I'm full of admiration when I hear
the lists of things that singers claim they'd do
in service of their love, but, so we're clear,
there's loads of stuff I wouldn't do for you.
I couldn't climb a mountain if I tried
nor walk five hundred miles – not even once –
or cross a river gorge, however wide,
so don't expect those tough, outdoorsy stunts.
I *could* lay down my life, I will admit,
by catching a grenade or other means,
but can't quite see the point: it's all a bit
dramatic, and I know you don't like scenes.
But don't assume my love's begun to pall;
I've written you this sonnet, after all.

Dawn Haiku

They watched the day break
and she said: see – this is why
we can't have nice things.

The Endless Dance

They follow one another round the house
and spot the things that aren't quite how they were.
Their marriage is a game of cat and mouse:
they follow one another round the house
in silence, each unnoticed by their spouse,
and put things back the way that they prefer.
They follow one another round the house
and spot the things that aren't quite as they were.

Boom

The thousand ways we've found to take away
another human life have not, combined,
kept pace with what is still the surest way
of making one we've managed yet to find.

.

What's in a Name?

written for the marriage of
Steve Callaghan and Juliet Clarke

As sure as dogs hate baths and cats and vets,
most English people naturally suppose
that well brought-up, unwedded Juliets
should properly be paired with Romeos.

But whilst they might be good for making grand
iambic declarations of their love –
you know the sort of thing: *How fair your hand!*
Oh, how I wish that I could be its glove! –

or saying that you're like some precious jewel
or lovely as a sweetly perfumed rose,
I'm sad to say there isn't, as a rule,
a lot to recommend most Romeos.

I'm sure that, to the people gathered here,
no matter what the world at large believes,
it couldn't be more eminently clear
that Juliets are better off with Steves.

A Juliet needs someone who'll be kind;
who'll pour her wine and cook her something nice;
who'll know her jokes are crap, but still won't mind;
who'll offer good sartorial advice;

who'll stay with her 'til they're both grey and old;
who'll maybe drive a fancy car as well –
in all these different ways it's Steves, I'm told,
not Romeos, who generally excel.

A love that's not disastrously ill-starred
seems on the whole to be a better bet;
let's leave the other version to the bard,
and raise a glass to Steve and Juliet.

Forever for Now

Your soulmate, from the moment you encounter them, will fill
your fundamental being with a love that's pure and strong;
your hearts will be entwined as one forever, or until
a soulmate either one of you likes better comes along.

The
Social
Ape

———

My Friend's Friend Is My Enemy

I know you'll call it jealousy;
it really isn't that.
I've tried my best, but honestly
your new friend's just a twat.
I hate him, but what irks me more
is now I can't quite tell
if he's your sole misjudgement or
if I'm a twat as well.

The Rule

The first and second times you haven't heard
what someone's said, put awkwardness aside
and ask them to repeat it, but the third
just smile and nod and hope that no one's died.

The In Crowd

There are hardly any gatherings or organised events
on the forty-something parent's social scene
more enjoyable or apt to bring reward in any sense
than an evening watching telly would have been.

Equal and Opposite

The bit of brain that tells me I should start
to wave when someone waves works slightly more
efficiently and quickly than the part
that tells me if we've ever met before.

An English Doorway

A first man stands aside and says politely: 'After you'.
'No, after you', a second man replies.
'No, really I insist', the first one says: 'Do come on through.'
And so it carries on 'til someone dies.

Jones's Law

For middle-class people,
contentment depends
on winning the envy
of middle-class friends.

In Memoriam

Though thousands of species of wondrous design
have tragically fallen extinct through Darwinian
selection or anthropogenic decline,
the one I miss most is the Unshared Opinion.

Conversation for Men

Just stand there politely and nod now and then
if they seem to be still in full swing,
and wait for a bit of a gap, which is when
you can say your more interesting thing.

Early Adopter

I try to stay ahead of modern trends;
while supermarket checkouts chose to wait,
relationships with nearly all my friends
went contactless in nineteen ninety-eight.

The Hardest Word

The usual English way of saying 'no'
is saying 'yes', not sleeping for the next
however long, convinced you'll have to go,
then pulling out belatedly by text.

Limited Company

My friendships have been very few;
the part that's most lamentable
is, if I'd only tried, those too
were probably preventable.

Silver Lining

Though vanishingly little recommends
(instead of watching telly with your spouse)
an evening playing host at home to friends,
at least it makes you tidy up the house.

Byproduct

A standard-issue Englishman, when run
from nine to five at full or fullish power,
discharges to the atmosphere a ton
of unrefined embarrassment per hour.

An Englishman's Castle

There's nothing that fills us with shock and despair
as fully as callers' neglecting
the unwritten rule that our doorbells are there
for visitors we were expecting.

The Water Cooler

To judge from all the conversation themes
I've heard throughout my working life so far,
I must have got the sort of face which screams:
I'd love you to describe how tired you are.

Dinner Time

When asked to come at eight, then, as a guide,
you ought to wait 'til quarter past to give
your hosts the chance to rush about and hide
the evidence of how they really live.

Boy Children

They compete and they jockey; they tussle and shout.
Are they fighting or playing? It's tricky to tell
as they tumble like cubs and get bundled about.
They compete and they jockey; they tussle and shout
as they grow and get grey, but they never grow out
of the vying to win, and it rarely ends well.
They compete and they jockey; they tussle and shout.
Are they fighting or playing? It's tricky to tell.

Easy Charm

It's easy, charm, when life keeps serving up
delightful things, and fortune fills your cup;
you'll truly know a man from his response
to learning that he can't have what he wants.

The Introverted Narcissist

You claim it's not a helpful combination;
it doesn't seem a lot to ask to me:
I merely crave the constant adulation
of people that I never want to see.

Suspended Sentence

A 'yes' ahead of time can feel as harmless as a 'no'
until you've felt the sudden, crushing sorrow
of something that you carelessly agreed to months ago
appearing on your schedule for tomorrow.

Digital Communication

In England, people rarely say the words: *'My hands are cold'*;
it's generally acknowledged that, in almost every case,
our point is made more clearly if we simply turn and hold
our fingers to another person's unsuspecting face.

The Reunion

It takes a furtive squinny at the name
that's pinned to your lapel for me to see,
behind the jowls and greying hair, the same
unpleasant git you always used to be.

Feedback Loop

You're keen to know how likely I would be to recommend
your car insurance offer to a relative or friend,
but whether I'd have friends at all would surely be in doubt
if car insurance deals were what I chose to talk about.

This
Writing
Life

———

Self-Critical

In case a critic ever feels inclined
to analyse my poetry, or – worse –
an English teacher tells their class to find
some deeper, hidden meaning in my verse

I thought I'd save them all a bit of time
and try to do it for them while I'm here
in thirty-two iambic lines that rhyme
(which isn't of importance, to be clear).

In stanza one, line one, you may detect
some harsh alliteration; honestly,
this wasn't for particular effect:
it's just the words I needed start with 'c'.

In fact, when certain sounds appear a lot
it almost always happens by mistake,
and hissing strings of sibilants are not
in any way suggestive of a snake.

And nowhere have I knowingly employed
enjambment as a way of placing stress
on certain words: at times, I can't avoid
a sentence spilling over, I confess.

The turtle dove (yes, this one) which we find
in stanza six is not a metaphor:
it's just a turtle dove which felt inclined
to steer a course this way, and nothing more.

I understand that humans like to see
significance which isn't really there,
but, in this case, I think it's down to me
to lay the truth behind these verses bare:

I thought my book was finalised, but still
my publisher as ever wanted more –
specifically, a poem that would fill
the space on pages sixty-three and four.

Under the Sun

I never write in libraries now;
I haven't done for years:
I find it too dispiriting
that almost every shelf
is full of books by bastards who
stole all my best ideas
before I'd even had the chance
to think of them myself.

Forgotten Masterpiece

This poem is a substitute for one
I thought of in the middle of the night,
awake still, having made my bathroom run,
but too asleep to sit, turn on the light
and find a pen and paper on the shelf
beside my bed to write it down. And so
I pulled the duvet up, and told myself
I'd leave it 'til the morning. And although
that poem could have been my *Grecian Urn*,
my *Kubla Khan*, my *Lonely as a Cloud*,
by daybreak it had gone; you live and learn.
I offer you this sonnet, though, unbowed,
and ask you to imagine in its stead
the finest lines of verse you've ever read.

Poets Haiku

If all the poets
were laid out end-to-end, it
wouldn't matter much.

<u>Light</u>? Verse

[1]Not weighty; [2]insubstantial; [3]lacking heft;
[4]inconsequential; [5]undemanding; [6]flimsy;
[7]of meagre value; [8]trivial; [9]bereft
of gravitas; [10]inane; [11]inclined to whimsy;
[12]devoid of substance; [13]evanescent; [14]trite;
[15]untaxing; [16]facile; [17]tame; [18]of little note;
[19]for children; [20]unsophisticated; [21]slight;
[22]not apt to make you want to slit your throat.

Definition Haiku

Prepositions are
those little words you mustn't
end sentences with.

The Absent-Minded Sonneteer

I find that, nowadays, I sometimes start
a sentence, but then, halfway through it, just . . .
I'm sure it must be due in no small part
to age, but, even so, it really must . . .
It happens far more often when I'm in . . .
My family and colleagues sometimes get . . .
Who wouldn't, to be fair? I can't begin . . .
Though, happily (touch wood) I haven't yet . . .
The worst it's ever been was when I was . . .
My wife just stood and stared at me and said . . .
Of course, I didn't understand because . . .
So, taking aim, she covered me in red . . .
To all of them, I'm deeply sorry for . . .
I'll really try to be a little more . . .

The Sincerest Form

I think it's just the rhyming poet's curse
that people who profess to like your books
send messages to say as much in verse,
and prove it's not as easy as it looks.

Efficiency Savings

You say you think
my sonnets could
use half the ink
and be as good
(or not much worse)
if I'd delete
from every verse
a few spare feet
but keep the rhyme
and metre in;
we'd save some time
and cash: win, win.
I'm not so sure
that less is more.

Cold Calling

The poet never used his two-bar heater;
there wasn't any money in the metre.

The Hindsight Oracles

Divining what the future brings
is hard; *courage, mon brave!*
It's easier to know that things
will happen once they have,
and forecasts made in retrospect
are almost always right.
When something comes to pass, affect
the sense you thought it might,
or mention that you saw the signs
which no one else could see,
and read the truth between the lines
with perspicacity.
Provided that your mantic take
post factum can be spun
to fifteen hundred words, you'll make
a journalist, my son.

Hierarchy of Nerds

By far the most prestigious epithet
for writing types is 'Nobel laureate',
and, twenty-thousand leagues or so below it,
by far the least is surely 'local poet'.

Life

Lessons

———

Wasted

We tend to mismanage abundant resources,
ignoring the obstinate truth
that they're finite; the clearest example, of course, is
the young and the days of their youth.

Victory Ode

When sportsmen win, they often cite their personal success
as proof that, with commitment, we can all achieve our dream,
imagining that no-one had explained as much, I guess,
to all those lazy losers on the opposition team.

Counter Factual

It's vital, if you want to watch your weight,
to learn the list of food that doesn't count:
the chips from someone else's bag or plate;
all snacks containing any trace amount
of fruit; the broken biscuits in the tin;
whole chocolate cakes, according to my wife,
provided that they're served in paper-thin
instalments, balanced sideways on the knife;
all liquids; roast potatoes picked by hand
from serving dishes; popcorn in the dark;
and anything that's eaten while you stand
within the open fridge door's glowing arc.
On unrelated matters, it transpires
That mirrors, belts and bathroom scales are liars.

Selfie Haiku

Vanity is just
insecurity that has
found an audience.

The Trap

We spend our adult lives, half-bored, half-stressed,
in pinstripe-suited drudgery to earn
enough to give our kids the very best
of starts in life, 'til, one day, in their turn,
they'll land good jobs, and work – half-bored, half-stressed –
in pinstripe-suited drudgery to earn
enough to give their kids the very best
of starts in life. And, no – we'll never learn.

Retrospective

Enormous things are better taken in
from far away; perspectives shift, somehow,
with distance. Thinking 'I was happy then'
is easier than 'I am happy now'.

The Bar

If nothing ever comes your way
but failures and frustrations,
the answer is to start each day
with lower expectations.

The Laundry Chair

If your clothes are all kept in a stratified pile
like the rocks of the new Pleistocene,
then, as long as you leave them alone for a while,
they'll emerge from it magically clean.

New Leaf

The smoking, the fry-ups, the beer by the crate
and the decades of flabby and pallid
inertia are magically wiped from the slate
if the last thing you ate was a salad.

Glossary

Al dente (from Italian)
is Middle Class for 'underdone'.

Inverse per Portion

for Tim C.

Those restaurants where the price of every course
is greater than my total private wealth
are always most inclined to serve me sauce
in thimblefuls I'm meant to pour myself.

All Consuming

It's simpler just to spend our time acquiring all the things
that other people seem to feel most envious about
than actually identify the stuff that truly brings
us happiness, so let's just all do that 'til life runs out.

Popping Out

If all the kitchen blackboards, post-it notes
and other aides-memoire of every ilk
were laid on end from here to John o'Groats,
I know I'd still forget the fucking milk.

Duel Carriageway

I know in the world there are far bigger worries,
like famines and children in need,
but lorries should not overtake other lorries
of almost identical speed.

Teaser

The trickiest in all the panoply
of life's unanswered questions great and small
is how those fruity sorts of herbal tea
can smell so good but taste of bugger all.

The To Don't List

The surest way to ascertain if any given task
in point of fact needs doing (as the wisest men intuit)
is not to seek your spouse or your superiors to ask,
but just to see what happens if you happen not to do it.

On the Mountain Top

How long I climbed, or how I knew
the path I cannot say,
but when the summit came in view
my tiredness ebbed away.
He sat, serene and sandal-less,
and, beckoning me near,
he said: 'To find true happiness
I wouldn't start from here'.

The Accidental Grown-Up

In adulthood, the key is how convincingly you fake
the air of one who hasn't just got older by mistake.

The Trouble with Happiness

It sometimes feels a simpler choice
to wish it over straight away
than live with that insistent voice:
you're bound to lose this all one day.

Freudenschade

Though criticism always stings a touch –
especially the sort that's bluntly phrased –
it somehow never rankles quite as much
as hearing other people being praised.

The

Art

of

Mediocrity

———

Unbition

You needn't aspire;
you don't have to strive;
it isn't essential
to captain the team.
The sort who aim higher
are no more alive:
re-leash your potential;
unfollow your dream.

Least Resistance

Though some suggest the most demanding challenges repay
most richly those prepared to struggle through them,
when things in life are difficult, it's really nature's way
of telling us we're not supposed to do them.

Tomorrow and Tomorrow

I think I just assumed that life would start
as soon as all the other jobs were done;
I wanted to believe it in my heart,
I think. I just assumed that life *would* start,
a hopeful understudy for the part
of me. I'd get my moment in the sun –
I think I just assumed that; life would start
as soon as all the other jobs were done.

Sticks and Stones

Whoever wrote the part that goes:
your words can never hurt
which nerds like me were taught to chant in chorus
must not have had a nemesis
who pinned them in the dirt
and beat them with an Oxford Schools Thesaurus.

Conspicuous Shallows

for Tim M.

My pitiful lack of discernible strengths,
you've clearly concluded, on balance
can best be explained by the diffident lengths
I've gone to in hiding my talents.

But it isn't the case, as you seem to presume,
that a bushel is hiding my light;
the reason it isn't dispelling the gloom
is just that it's not very bright.

I haven't got depths that are hidden for sure,
or a trumpet I choose not to blow;
there's less here than first meets the eye and not more,
and only one string to my bow.

My talents are more like the slow-punctured tyre
on a bike than the keel of a ship,
and what you can see is the iceberg entire
and not, as you think, just the tip.

But the rumour I'm keeping my genius quiet
has spread far and wide, thanks to you,
and the best part of all is, the more I deny it,
the more people think that it's true.

The Subs' Bench Triolet

I hope that someone else gets hurt –
not badly, though, you understand.
But, seeing as my loins are girt,
I hope that someone else gets hurt
who won't mind lending me his shirt
before he gets his ankle scanned.
I hope that someone else gets hurt.
Not badly, though. You understand.

The Cookbook

To make a change from ready meals and tins,
I'm trying something cooked from scratch today.
'The night before . . .' the recipe begins;
I close the book and order take-away.

Minding My Own Busyness

My weekday brain was full of all the jobs that I would do
as soon as I had time, but as the weekend hours slide past
it dawns on me the problem – I suspect I always knew –
was less a lack of time and more a lack of being arsed.

Laurel and Hardly

A single bay leaf added to the pot
then carefully extracted makes me feel
a bit more like a grown-up cook, but not
the slightest bit of difference to my meal.

I'm Lost Too

Celebrities and motivation gurus never seem
to tell you what to follow if you haven't got a dream.

Stitching Time

I wish that I could sew together extra, patchwork days
from all the little scraps of time I've wasted down the years –
the idle minutes here and there imagining the ways
I'd spend the Lotto jackpot, or researching new careers
I knew I'd never follow, or rehearsing in my head
the perfect lines I should have used in arguments of old,
or scrolling through the channels then just going up to bed
or making cups of tea that I'd forget and let go cold.
I'd know I ought to use my salvaged time to undertake
some virtuous endeavour, as I'm sure would better men,
but balls to self-improvement or the difference I could make:
I'd simply like to have the chance to waste it all again.

Worst of Both

I'm almost impressed that, to such a degree
on dozens of various fronts,
my adulthood manages somehow to be
both boring and stressful at once.

Reality

My life is not a TV show
but, if it were, my fear is
the ratings would be far too low
to get a second series.

Sunday Jobs

For painting the skirtings or making a shelf
or mending the tyre on a bike
I'm fine with the concept of Do It Yourself –
it's Do It *My*self I don't like.

The Contender

We're happier to tell ourselves that life would now be good
if only we had made some different choice than to admit
that all the other roads we saw diverging in that wood
would probably have led us somewhere shitter, or as shit.

Overthinking

———

cogito ergo . . . *hmm*

My constant second-guessing and imagining the worst
can cause my life's machinery to jam,
and everything needs time built-in for agonising first;
I overthink, therefore I under-am.

Too Much Information

It's more or less impossible to learn
– whatever your existing state of health –
the symptoms of an illness and, in turn,
not instantly develop them yourself.

Not Guilty

I've got a particular walk that I use
whenever policemen are near –
the insouciant gait of a man who eschews
misdemeanours (or that's the idea).
A glimpse of high-vis or a blue flashing light,
and I'm instantly rather too keen
to project, 'til I'm sure that I'm well out of sight,
an unburdened and innocent mien,
as I saunter deliberately, taking my time,
and I strain every sinew to act
in a nonchalant way, and conceal all the crime
that I haven't committed, in fact.

The Truth Will Out

They say that secrets always come to light
eventually, like bodies in the snow,
but (even though they seem convinced they're right)
I cannot help but wonder how they know.

The Lottery Ticket

As soon as I check, I'll discover for sure
that I haven't, alas, won a share
of the jackpot. I'll leave it; I like it much more
being Schrödinger's millionaire.

Peripeteia

I've heard enough and read enough
of happy men brought low
that sometimes, as I lie awake at night,
I wish that all the awful stuff
would happen quickly so
I didn't have to worry that it might.

On and Off

I wonder how much time we'd save in all
if, when we bought a house, we tried each switch
to see which did the landing, stairs and hall,
and bothered to remember which was which.

Darkest before the Dawn

My brain: It's 3 am. We need more sleep.
My brain as well: This urgently requires
a comprehensive audit of our deep
anxieties and innermost desires.

The Enemy Within

There isn't an occasion when our trembling hearts are filled
(for all that our insouciant demeanour might belie it)
with such acute alarm as when a rumble starts to build
from somewhere in our tummies in a room that's fallen quiet.

Clueless

I chew my biro lid. I frown.
I can't decipher seven down.
I frown. I'm at a total loss.
I can't make sense of four across.
I'm lost. I can't make head or tail
Of thirteen down. I try. I fail.
Is six across an anagram?
Would *MARMOT* fit for seven . . . damn.
By now, of course, I could have done
three-quarters of the easy one –
but that would make me feel less bright
than getting none of these ones right.

Half-Glass Haiku

I woke up today
feeling quite optimistic.
Always a bad sign.

Bum Note

I've pondered it a lot, and yet
I still can't solve the riddle
of why it's called a bottom when
it's clearly in the middle.

Survival of the Defeatist

My mother takes the view that, if disasters tend to strike
when people least expect them, it's incumbent on us all
to spend our days from dawn 'til dusk and restless nights alike
concertedly expecting something dreadful to befall.

How You Play the Game

However hard an Englishman is minded to contend
to win the prize for which his peers are vying,
it's nothing like the effort that he's willing to expend
to look as though he isn't really trying.

The
March
of
Progress

———

Typo

There's nothing more obscure to human sight
nor glaringly apparent, I'd contend,
than any e-mail typo, grave or slight,
a moment either side of pressing 'Send'.

Rubik's Cubicle

for Daviona

You're likelier by far to get
                  a full and frank admission
that they've buggered up the country
                  from a British politician,
or a message from your children
                  that is wholly un-sarcastic,
or a present from a Kinder Egg
                  that isn't made of plastic,
or a comprehensive, worked-through proof
                  for Fermat's final theorem
from the Leeds United first team
                  and the men who stand and cheer them,
or a quiz on soaps and 80s pop
                  from Intertel or Mensa
than you are to get the paper
                  from a toilet roll dispenser.

The One-Legged Stool

Our kids should all learn science then
get science-based careers,
our leaders cry, while dreaming of the day
when concert halls are full of rows
of software engineers
just sitting there and watching no-one play.

One for Luck

What reckless fool or witless dunce
who flies at life half-cocked
would press their key fob only once
and think the car was locked?

Content & Contentment

I don't know when we started to confuse
with pleasure the emotion that derives
from seeing photographs and hearing news
of other people's stupid happy lives,
but everybody's mood would be improved,
I'm sure, if all those smugly gurning scenes
of prosperous contentment were removed
from websites and from lifestyle magazines.
I'd rather see a glossy, five-page spread
of someone unsuccessful and their spouse,
or maybe a regretful newlywed
at home inside their cramped, untidy house,
and, oh! how glad I'd be to go online
to gawp at lives as second-rate as mine.

Mod Cons

The fact that I can never work the plug
in modern sinks would irk me more, perhaps,
if somehow I imagined, like a mug,
I stood a chance of turning on the taps.

Labour Saving

Necessity is said to be
the mother of invention,
which may be true, but simplifies things rather;
increasingly it seems to me
we also ought to mention
that laziness is usually the father.

Between the Lines

Our English email software ought to be
in most respects entirely orthodox,
with subject-line, address and bcc,
but also have an extra 'subtext' box.

Rate the World

Just one more thing: we'd love to know
how well we did before you go,
so rate this film and rate that book
and rate your meal and rate our cook,
and rate the stuff we sold to you,
and rate the bloke who brought it too,
and rate your journey, rate the driver,
rate the destination – either
rate them now or rate them later –
rate it all, then rate the rater.
Rate the land and sea and sky;
rate everything before you die,
then rate the priest and undertaker,
rate the gates and rate your maker
once you've met; you needn't show him.
Rate the lot. Now rate this poem.

Mutually Assured Distraction

As their planet died
they were arguing about
a gold and white* dress.

---

* *blue and black*

Cap and Capitalism

The argument that, by itself, the Market can restrain
its lust for growth will surely best be made
when razor manufacturers make adverts to explain
they're not convinced we need another blade.

Bad Form

written for the 'How To Hold a Grudge' podcast

We'd quickly need to reappraise existing social norms
if people ever learned to interact like online forms,
as, every time we spoke, our interlocutors would shout:
'THAT'S NOT A VALID SENTENCE!' as we rushed to spit it out.

And if, through all the barracking, we made it to the end
of something we were saying, then our algorithmic friend
would frown and shake their head and make us go back through the list
of everything we'd said and fill in sections that we'd missed.

And if we had a later conversation, we would find
that everything we'd told them had completely slipped their mind;
they'd ask us all the questions that they'd asked before, and then
they'd shout: 'INVALID SENTENCE!' as we answered them again.

Bacon Pack Haiku

You don't need scissors.
You just peel back this little . . .
I'll get the scissors.

Vanity 1.0

for Sarah

Before there was the Internet,
when you were not yet born,
we carried sacks of photographs,
all dog-eared at the ends,
of everywhere we'd visited,
each outfit that we'd worn
and every plate of food we'd made,
to show to all our friends.

The Goldfish

To help myself remember little things,
I message me@ageingbrain.com
then, half a second later, when it pings
think: 'Ooh, a text. I wonder who it's from?'

True / False

written for the 'How To Hold a Grudge' podcast

The fire alarms of England meet with various responses,
but none is quite as prevalent as studied nonchalance is,
and working on, unruffled, through the caterwauling racket
as though it were the rustling of a Chocolate Hobnob packet.

The feistier among us, more inclined to vent our feelings
and tut and sigh and pace and stare accusingly at ceilings,
type strongly worded missives while the sirens go on screeching
explaining all the working rights directives that they're breeching.

Still others, who have slightly more pragmatic dispositions,
take steps to counteract the most cacophonous emissions
with jumpers tied round sounders or their headphones turned up higher.
The only thing that no one does is think that there's a fire.

Now and Then

Whenever they put footage on TV
of news events from years ago, it's weird
to think that, at the time, we couldn't see
how quaintly out of date it all appeared.

The Autophage

The human race invented tools, then ever more machines
to do the things they'd always had to do themselves before.
The last of their inventions could invent things; then, it seems,
the world that they'd invented didn't need them anymore.

Dialogue Box

written for the 'How To Hold a Grudge' podcast

I haven't met a human being yet
who's shown as much concern or been as frank
in seeking to protect me from regret
as emails when I've left the subject blank.

Algorithm and Blues

We worry that machines are so
intelligent, they'll end
humanity's enduring reign
at evolution's peak;
intelligent machines, meanwhile,
still rush to recommend
new sandwich grills to people who
bought sandwich grills last week.

Two
Tribes

The Unlightenment

We can't be arsed with tomes and tracts
by boffin-headed minions:
we trust our guts, not nerds and quacks;
we can't be arsed with tomes and tracts;
the world should simply change its facts
to fit with our opinions.
We can't be arsed with tomes and tracts
by boffin-headed minions.

Manifesto

Our view that inequality
is wrong will never waver
(unless, by serendipity,
it's working in our favour).

Dimocracy

The ancient Greeks, millennia ago
devised a hundred-generations-long
political experiment to show
that slightly more than half of us are wrong.

The Barrier

Of all the thoughts that stand and wait to gain
admission through the turnstile of your brain
– it's narrow and the queue is slow and long –
the very last is: 'Maybe I was wrong'.

The Political Passive

We didn't make mistakes; mistakes were made.
We didn't speak untruths; untruths were spoken.
We didn't pay our friends; our friends were paid.
We didn't break our pledges; they were broken.
We didn't flout the rules; the rules were flouted.
We didn't have affairs; affairs were had.
We didn't spout that bile, but bile was spouted –
and, look, we understand that things look bad.
Our country's been let down, without a doubt,
and just like all of you, we've had enough.
We'll start to fix it once we've figured out
which useless pricks keep doing all this stuff.

Fool's Gold

No tabloid hack or partisan MP
or online troll or bloody-minded youth
has yet pulled off that verbal alchemy
of yelling their opinion into truth.

Tomb of the Keyboard Warrior

O, here lies a hero of online debate!
He fearlessly made up his mind in a second
and, quoting some facts that he'd heard from his mate,
he died on the hill of the stuff that he reckoned.

Vox Populi

Our vote's the voice our forebears fought so bravely to attain,
and when we draw that cross in ballpoint ink
it serves to swell the volume of democracy's refrain:
We're idiots – don't ask us what we think.

An Atheist's Prayer

O, keep me from temptation, Lord above,
lest in my hour of suffering and grief
the promise of eternal life and love
should undermine my steadfast disbelief.

The Only Constant

The merits of change are so often extolled
by a vocal and passionate few
who've only considered the cons of the old
and only the pros of the new.

Two Tribes

The others on the 'net seem sure
we'd get it if we weren't so dumb.
Although we've never met before
the others on the 'net seem sure
the angrier they get the more
persuasive all their views become.
The others on the 'net seem sure
we'd get it if we weren't so dumb.

No Right Turn

We'd rather go on suffering the pain of our mistakes,
pretending this was really what we wanted all along,
and promising to see it through, no matter what it takes,
than face the mild discomfort of admitting we were wrong.

Inventing the Enemy

There's a dangerous enemy tribe who refuse
to see reason, or so we've been told,
and the people like us are incensed at the views
we've decided they probably hold.

On Conflict

When fractious children start to fight
and both begin to mither,
demanding that we choose who's right,
the answer can be: neither.

Up and Down

To be forced to live forever
with the sort of clientele
who would make it into heaven
would be my idea of hell.

High
Days
and
Holidays

———

Easter Story

I didn't eat chocolate at all during Lent,
but all of the Toblerone Minis since then
and bags of Maltesers for breakfast have meant
my body mass index has risen again.

Tourist Trap Haiku

Strangers get caught in
the backgrounds of photos like
insects in amber.

The Christmas Message

The angel of the Lord appeared on high
to certain lowly shepherds, and decreed
that men should bicker, over-eat and buy
a load of crap they didn't really need.

The Invention of Gift-Wrap

Those wrapping paper pioneers of old had somehow seen
the future, and had understood, no matter what it took,
there ought to be, however short, an interval between
receiving any gift and finding out it was a book.

26. XII

There used to be a feast called Boxing Day
the origins of which are now unknown
when relatives would all agree to stay
a bit too long in one another's homes,
and food they'd cooked and cooled the day before
and clingfilmed onto plates was offered up
with weary prompts to take a little more
and maybe have another glass or cup.
To decorate their homes, beside each chair
they'd leave a pile of hardback books and socks
(which none of them would ever read or wear)
and fold up shiny paper in a box,
and in this way their gods of rubbish, cheese
and bickering were annually appeased.

The New Year

We usher in the timid year
at midnight to the sound
of plastic fanfares, drunken cheers,
inchoate brawls and jilted tears,
as dropped kebabs and half-drunk beers
lie littering the ground.
It's clear how, witnessed all at once,
this scene might cause offence,
– this cavalcade of coarse affronts,
unseemly rows and booze-fuelled stunts –
and why the year then spends twelve months
demanding recompense.

Vive la Résolution

I go out jogging twice a week, come rain or snow or ice –
the week that ends on January the eighth, to be precise.

Variations on a Theme

I mentioned once in passing years ago
how much I liked a duck. I'm not sure why,
but seemingly it stuck with you, and so
next birthday, you dispatched to me a tie
emblazoned with a skein of ducks in flight.
'I hope you like the ducks!' your message cried.
And then, when Christmas came, you sent some bright
green socks with ducks embroidered up the side.
And every year since then, it's been the same:
a pair of mallard cufflinks; duck-themed mugs;
an actual duck you sponsored in my name;
some matching, duck-shaped milk and water jugs.
And now it's been so long it would be rude
to say I meant I liked them more as food.

House Rules

'We save the china cups for best';
she told us so with solemn force.
In case of uninvited guests,
we saved the china cups for best.
I'm sure they would have been impressed,
but no one ever came, of course.
We saved the china cups for best.
She told us so with solemn force.

Poem for an Odd-Numbered Birthday

I might not stay out drinking past eleven,
and maybe my libido has decreased,
but now I've reached the age of forty-seven,
I'm in my prime mathematically at least.

Ending

Dead Set

A subject to which I've devoted some thought is
the posture I'd choose for my own *rigor mortis*;
whatever position my heirs see me off in,
I hope that it calls for a custom-built coffin.

The Balance

On gravestones, they ought to divide into two
and display in a table or grid
the things that we always intended to do
and the things that we actually did.

Don't Pity the Widow

Don't pity the widow who shops by herself
then buses back home to the house that they shared,
where family photographs propped on a shelf
remind her of days when she stood, auburn-haired,
beside him. Don't pity the widow who spends
as long as she can in the park every day
and chatters to strangers as though they were friends
or sits on a bench, watching families play.
Don't pity the widow who puts down the phone,
or turns off the telly, then quietly shuts
the door to the bedroom she sleeps in alone:
her husband was rich, and she hated his guts.

exegi monumentum

We write our names upon the sand
as, all the while, the tide comes in.
We use whatever comes to hand
to write our names upon the sand,
then, stepping back a pace, we stand
admiringly, with hand on chin.
We write our names upon the sand
and all the while the tide comes in.

Horatian Haiku

I try to live each
day as if it were my last:
in bed, on a drip.

Judgement

The prophet of doom could conclusively say
as he gazed at the sun's dying light
that the end of the world was a small price to pay
for definitive proof he was right.

Shadows

Our tragedies are born the day we're born,
but, eager not to introduce themselves
too soon, they bide their time and watch us grow,
make choices, fall in love, and find our way.
They follow closely everywhere we go,
down side roads, lanes and aisles, until, one day
(when, on a whim, we're tidying the lawn
or making tea or putting up some shelves)
they take us by the arm and grip it tight
and whisper in our ear that something's wrong,
or send someone on their behalf to knock,
or telephone us strangely late at night,
and, even as our throats choke dry with shock,
we understand we've known them all along.

Bequest

In equal shares I leave to you
the fun I should have had
and living I forgot to do.
Don't waste them, boys. Love, Dad

Wake

We talk of our shock, and the things we can learn
from his life, as we haltingly search
for a point, and ignore that we'll all get our turn
in the box at the front of the church.

Falling Upwards

Exactly as you seldom see their bodies on the ground
for all the living birds that fill the sky,
you rarely read of arseholes in obituaries, I've found;
I guess we all fall upwards when we die.

Half Life

The end draws nightly closer by degrees;
The end draws nightly closer by.
The end draws nightly close.
The end draws nigh.
The end.

Last Words

I've noticed – though their authors' reputations aren't diminished –
The greatest works of literature are often left un

Acknowledgements

I am inordinately grateful to Jamie Hodder-Williams and everyone at Bedford Square Publishing for getting behind this book. Jamie's unwavering belief in my poems has meant a great deal, and his calm, intelligent and tactful guidance has improved the book significantly. He has been a pleasure to work with. Thanks to Polly Halsey, who remained a model of patience and calm throughout the editing process, in spite of my indecision, last minute changes and incessant wittering about metre and line breaks, and also to David Wardle for the cover design and Anastasia Boama-Aboagye for marketing.

Huge thanks, too, are due to my agent, Peter Straus, for throwing his not-inconsiderable clout behind a little book of slightly silly poems.

I remain enormously indebted to Sophie Hannah for her tireless and incredibly generous support over more than a decade, and for her clear-headed and unerring advice. I am grateful too for the support she has given me through the *How To Hold a Grudge* podcast (for which three poems in this collection were originally written).

Warm thanks must also go to Matt Kelly and Steve Anglesey at *The New European* for giving me what must be one of the very few regular gigs in the country writing short, silly poems, which is a total joy. A number of the poems in this collection were first published as part of the 'Nic Aubury's Four-Line Poem' feature.

I remain very grateful to Luke Wright and Nasty Little

Press, who, a dozen years ago or more, published early versions of a handful of poems that have been re-worked here. Without Luke's early, enthusiastic support, my further forays into poetry would never have happened, so in a very real sense this is all his fault.

I am also extremely grateful to my oldest pal, Brian Schofield, whose home-made 'World's Median Dad' mug inspired the poem of the same name. His is the only joke that I have knowingly stolen in writing this book, a theft which he was very gracious to allow.

Many thanks, too, to Juliet and Steve Callaghan for allowing me to re-work and reprint here a poem that was written for, and read at, their wedding.

Immeasurable thanks, as ever, go to my mum and dad for their unstinting love and support, and for sharing with me a good number of the foibles and neuroses which have given rise to these poems. Thanks, too, to my sister for always being my least objective critic and most vocal cheerleader.

Finally, thanks and boundless love to Tom, Jamie, Fred and Emma, for indulging me and for enduring the igno-miny of having a poet in the family.

Nic Aubury

About the Author

Nic Aubury grew up in the Midlands, where he spent most of his time trying to get girls to laugh at his jokes. Then he went to university where he met a girl whose jokes made him laugh. Now they have three sons, some friends they keep meaning to call, and a bag of salad rotting slowly in their fridge. Nic has worked in advertising and teaching. He started writing poems by mistake.

@NicAubury

Bedford Square Publishers

Bedford Square Publishers is an independent publisher of fiction and non-fiction, founded in 2022 in the historic streets of Bedford Square London and the sea mist shrouded green of Bedford Square Brighton.

Our goal is to discover irresistible stories and voices that illuminate our world.

We are passionate about connecting our authors to readers across the globe and our independence allows us to do this in original and nimble ways.

The team at Bedford Square Publishers has years of experience and we aim to use that knowledge and creative insight, alongside evolving technology, to reach the right readers for our books. From the ones who read a lot, to the ones who don't consider themselves readers, we aim to find those who will love our books and talk about them as much as we do.

We are hunting for vital new voices from all backgrounds – with books that take the reader to new places and transform perceptions of the world we live in.

Follow us on social media for the latest Bedford Square Publishers news.

𝕏 @bedsqpublishers
facebook.com/bedfordsq.publishers/
@bedfordsq.publishers

https://bedfordsquarepublishers.co.uk/